Summary and Analysis of

GRIT

The Power of Passion
and Perseverance

Based on the Book
by Angela Duckworth

WORTH BOOKS
SMART SUMMARIES

All rights reserved, including without limitation the right to reproduce this book or any portion thereof in any form or by any means, whether electronic or mechanical, now known or hereinafter invented, without the express written permission of the publisher.

This Worth Books book is based on the 2016 ebook edition of *Grit* by Angela Duckworth, published by Scribner.

Summary and analysis copyright © 2017 by Open Road Integrated Media, Inc.

ISBN: 978-1-5040-4676-3

Worth Books
180 Maiden Lane
Suite 8A
New York, NY 10038
www.worthbooks.com

WORTH BOOKS
SMART SUMMARIES

Worth Books is a division of Open Road Integrated Media, Inc.

The summary and analysis in this book are meant to complement your reading experience and bring you closer to a great work of nonfiction. This book is not intended as a substitute for the work that it summarizes and analyzes, and it is not authorized, approved, licensed, or endorsed by the work's author or publisher. Worth Books makes no representations or warranties with respect to the accuracy or completeness of the contents of this book.

Contents

Context	1
Overview	3
Summary	5
Cast of Characters	23
Direct Quotes and Analysis	27
Trivia	33
What's That Word?	37
Critical Response	41
About Angela Duckworth	45
For Your Information	47
Bibliography	49

Context

In our current educational and workplace cultures, where people are judged by the narrow standards of IQ and family income, respectively, psychologist and MacArthur Fellow Angela Duckworth introduces two brand-new predictors of success: passion and perseverance. Duckworth contends that these two qualities, as opposed to innate talent, are the real foundation of accomplishment, opening the door and giving hope to individuals of diverse socioeconomic backgrounds and abilities. Together, she defines these qualities as "grit."

Building on the work of many other noted psychologists and researchers, Duckworth details what grit is and how one can get it, grow it, and encourage it in others.

SUMMARY AND ANALYSIS

Duckworth's TED Talk on grit has been viewed more than 8 million times, and her book was an immediate bestseller, spawning articles and think pieces in outlets as varied as *Slate* and *Scientific American*.

Overview

Angela Duckworth, who holds degrees in neuroscience and psychology, offers evidence-based research to argue that the qualities she deems to be part of "grit"—determination, resilience, passion, and perseverance—may matter more in shaping career and academic success than intellect or innate ability. Luck, opportunity, and ability matter as well, of course, but without grit, they are not enough. What does grit entail? Committing to something as if it is a life mission, with a full heart and love for the work; getting back up when you are knocked down; and sticking to a goal like glue. These traits are far more likely to help you get ahead than being the smartest person in the room. Those with grit strive to complete whatever they set out to do despite any pain or disappointment that may occur along the way.

The two key elements of grit are passion and perseverance. The main components of passion are interest and purpose, while perseverance is made up of practice and hope. Often passion gets lost in the equation, but Duckworth makes the distinction between sticking to something out of fear of failure and getting up day after day because of an innate interest in the endeavor and a general optimism that it can be achieved.

Duckworth goes beyond a definition of this theory to discuss how to cultivate the qualities of grit, providing concrete steps that can help readers become gritty. She shows grit at work in the examples of West Point cadets, dedicated athletes, and Scripps National Spelling Bee winners. And because everyone has the ability to grow and leverage grit on his chosen path to success, she helps readers find and develop it within themselves.

Summary

Preface

The author shares the fact that she grew up in a Chinese immigrant household with a father who prized intellect and talent above anything else. There was very little that Duckworth felt she could do to impress him. Her father frequently told her, "You know, you're no genius," and she internalized these put-downs. In school, she didn't test highly enough for the gifted and talented program. Never feeling like she was particularly brilliant or skilled, she got by with hard work, dedication, and a commitment to everything she took on, eventually graduating from excellent universities. But it was only when she won a MacArthur Fellowship—often called a "genius grant"—that she had her light-bulb moment. She looked back on what had gotten her to where she was—a distinguished professor of psychology and a scholar who had attended some of the top schools in the world—and realized that so-called "genius" had little to do with it. It was about character. She knew she had a calling and she challenged herself every day. "I may not be the smartest person in the room, but I strive to be the grittiest," she says.

Part I: What Grit Is and Why It Matters

Chapter 1: Showing Up

One of the most important characteristics of grit is refusing to quit. A gritty person shows up and sticks to the task at hand, no matter how hard it gets. It's that "never give up" attitude that determines who stays in the race. This chapter starts with a description of what West Point cadets go through in their first months at the military academy. They've already reached high levels of academic achievement, with top scores on their SATs and ACTs. They've trained hard and passed the required physicals. They've gotten the glowing recommendations of members of congress and senators and beaten out more than 14,000 applicants in the admissions process. Only 1,200 are admitted and enrolled, and yet one in five of these high achievers drops out before graduation. In fact, most of those who quit do so during their first summer, when they must go through a rigorous seven-week training program known as Beast Barracks—or just Beast—with days of drills, marching, and calisthenics that begin at 5 a.m. and end at 10 p.m.

For generations, psychologists and West Point leaders had struggled to figure out why some of these impressive people got through that period and others quit. Examining what it takes to make it through Beast, and many other career challenges, Duckworth develops the Grit Scale, a test designed to rate the level of perseverance and passion of an individual. In 2004, West Point cadets were given the test, asked to agree or disagree with statements such as "I finish whatever I begin," and "[My] interests change from year to year." By the end of the Beast training, a pattern emerged: Those with the grittiest answers made it through.

Need to Know: The Grit Scale became an accurate predictor of success when applied to employees in sales, a profession where rejection is a daily, if not hourly, experience. It also worked for juniors in a Chicago public high school, Green Berets, and Scripps National Spelling Bee contestants. The conclusion? "Our potential is one thing. What we do with it is quite another."

SUMMARY AND ANALYSIS

Chapter 2: Distracted by Talent

Examining some of the earliest treatises on what makes some people successful and others not, Duckworth cites a discussion between the founder of evolutionary theory, Charles Darwin, and his half cousin, Francis Galton. In 1869, Galton wrote a paper concluding that high achievers were remarkable for their combination of ability, zeal, and capacity for hard labor. Darwin agreed (although he actually considered natural talent to be the least important aspect of success). In 1907, psychologist William James furthered this hypothesis, making the observation that there is a gap between our potential and our achievements—we have the inner resources and intellect but we don't work at the optimum level. Those few who do put in the effort to push their innate powers to the outer extremes, however, are very successful.

Duckworth's point is that this notion is nothing new, and yet we've allowed ourselves to become sidetracked by talent, favoring the gifted over the strivers. She first noticed the importance of striving after she quit her job at McKinsey, a global management consulting firm, to teach middle school math to inner-city students. She noticed that the kids who didn't grasp the mathematical formulas right away ultimately fared better in terms of grades than many of the more naturally gifted students. This surprised her, leading her to examine why those with less natural aptitude would excel. The pattern she noticed was that the high achievers showed up every day, focused and prepared. They were less distracted by their classmates or by what was going on outside the window. When they didn't understand something the first time around, they tried again and again, coming for extra help at lunchtime.

Need to Know: Aptitude does not guarantee achievement.

Chapter 3: Effort Counts Twice

We have a built-in bias that favors talent and intellect. But by overemphasizing talent, we've underemphasized not only the importance of effort, but also of the dozens of small or ordinary skills that can amount to extraordinary achievement. Duckworth refers to a study of competitive swimmers by sociologist Dan Chambliss, a swimmer himself. After six years of interviewing, watching, and traveling with swimmers and coaches at all levels, from the local swim club to a top team made up of future Olympians, Chambliss discovered that, beyond having families with means and access to swimming pools and coaches, it was the thousands of hours these swimmers spent practicing that made them stand out. While these incremental efforts seem mundane, the success of the swimmers bolsters the argument that, by cultivating grit, anyone has the potential for greatness if he is willing to spend years refining the many individual elements that can add up to a single flawless performance. Of course, you can't train for certain anatomical differences that may help an athlete or natural aptitudes that may help an artist. Nevertheless, we tend to overestimate talent's role. We do this because it lets us off the hook and allows us to relax into the status quo. Those who have grit don't allow themselves this luxury.

Need to Know: Luck and innate talent are incomplete explanations for success. Effort factors into the equation twice, not once, because it builds a skill and makes that skill more productive.

Chapter 4: How Gritty Are You?

Grit is about much more than simply working hard on a project or endeavor; it is about stamina. Whether in business, academia, a profession, or a vocation, there are no shortcuts to excellence. Solving the problem, building real expertise, developing a product, or completing a project that has value to others takes far more time than most people imagine. Grit means not only falling in love with something enough to commit your all to it, but also staying in love with it. In order to help her readers rate their grittiness, Duckworth provides an example of a Grit Scale, on which readers can rate their responses, from one to five, to statements such as:

- New ideas and projects sometimes distract me from previous ones.
- I am a hard worker.
- I have overcome setbacks to conquer an important challenge.

To drill down deeper, readers can also rate themselves on the two components of grit: passion and perseverance. (By *passion*, Duckworth means intensity, not obsession or infatuation.) Most score a little higher on perseverance than passion, although you can't have one without the other.

Need to Know: Grit is mutable, and it can be cultivated. People can keep themselves on track by setting a hierarchy of goals. You know you have grit when you are able to hold the same top-level goal for a long time.

Chapter 5: Grit Grows

Whether it's generosity or talent, compassion or IQ, every human trait is influenced by genetics, or nature.

SUMMARY AND ANALYSIS

But nurture plays a huge role, too. Scientists have been studying identical and fraternal twins for decades to try to understand the inheritability of traits. To this effect, the Grit Scale was administered to more than 2,000 pairs of teenage twins in the United Kingdom, finding that there is an estimated 27% heritability of perseverance and 20% of passion. These results prove that, while some grit variability in the general population can be explained as genetics, most of it is attributable to experience. This means that the deck is not stacked against anyone.

Age does not limit us, either. In fact, according to dozens of studies, most people become more conscientious, confident, caring, and calm with life experience. Perhaps grit is a function of our particular cultural era, or we get grittier as we get older. Either way, it's not a fixed character trait, and it can be cultivated by understanding where we are today, changing our patterns of self-talk, zeroing in on weaknesses, engaging in the daily discipline of trying to do things better, and digging deeper to find purpose, because what ripens passion is the conviction that your work matters.

Need to Know: Complacency is the enemy of grit. A paragon of grit doesn't say, "This will never work," or "I might as well give up." Instead, she says, "Whatever it is, I want to improve," regardless of his level of skill or accomplishment.

Part II: Growing Grit from the Inside Out

Chapter 6: Interest

All the great achievers point to one quality that drives them: passion. They love what they do, and work doesn't seem like work because they are excited when they wake up every morning. Their professions are callings rather than jobs.

But that exhortation to "follow your passion" was not something that Duckworth, or many of her contemporaries, heard from her family while growing up. Like many, she was encouraged to find a safe, stable profession that prioritized security and financial reward over fulfillment. But research clearly shows that people are more satisfied and motivated in their jobs when they fit with their personal interests. They also perform better: Visionaries and big-picture thinkers don't thrive when they are managing logistically complicated projects, and those who love dealing with people aren't at their best when they work alone at computers all day. Clearly, interest is another critical component of the grit factor—and something that more than two-thirds of adults are missing. That's why many feel disengaged at work, according to a 2014 Gallup Poll. Desire, passion, and the strength of our interest: This is the fuel that fires up grit. And yet, it's not always immediately obvious what what our passions are.

Need to Know: Accept that it may take years to find your true passion. Julia Child didn't realize her true calling until middle age. Award-winning chef Marc Vetri was more interested in music than food as a teen.

Chapter 7: Practice

High-achieving gritty people generally stick with their commitments longer than others, whether they are National Spelling Bee winners, PGA golfers, or Scrabble champions. It is not only this persistence that makes a difference, though. We all know plenty of people who do things for decades and only achieve middling levels of competence. The difference is that gritty people are constantly striving to better themselves. Duckworth points to the Japanese term *kaizen*, which means to resist the plateau of arrested development—literally, "continuous improvement." Extremely successful people all have this innate desire to excel beyond their already notable talents or achievements. It is a never-ending desire to do better and a positive state of mind in which one looks forward and wants to grow. The author cites examples such as a study that compared violinists at a German music academy. Those musicians who reached the highest level of skill had put in a thousand hours of practice per year, while those who never achieved that level practiced far less. She quotes the choreographer Martha Graham, who said, "It takes about ten years to make a mature dancer."

Need to Know: The trick is not to log long hours of practice so much as to practice deliberately, with the set goal of getting better at a particular task while keeping track of performance.

Chapter 8: Purpose

Purpose, the other component of passion, means doing something with intent and for the well-being of others. Duckworth cites the example of Alex Scott as someone who was purpose-driven in her quest for grit. Alex was diagnosed with neuroblastoma when she was a year old, and spent her early childhood in and out of hospitals. She told her mother she was going to run a lemonade stand when she got out of the hospital, and she did, raising $2,000 so that her doctors could help other sick children. By the time she passed away at the age of eight, she'd inspired so many to do the same that she raised more than $1 million. The foundation her family started to uphold her legacy, Alex's Lemonade Stand, has raised more than $100 million for cancer research.

SUMMARY AND ANALYSIS

It is common to start out with a self-oriented interest, develop it with practice, and then integrate that work into something that serves others. This correlates to psychologist Benjamin Bloom's study on the three-phase progression of how people develop in a field, from the "early years," when they start based on interest, to "the middle years," when they focus on practice, to the "later years," when mature, gritty people find larger purposes and meanings. Duckworth posits that the grittier the person, the more likely he is to view his job as a calling, something that is beneficial to the world. She explains this by referencing a parable about three bricklayers: One bricklayer thinks of himself as laying bricks, the second considers himself to be constructing a church, and the third believes he is building a house of God. The third bricklayer, Duckworth would say, has grit.

Need to Know: There is no inherent conflict in doing something for your own good that is also for the good of others.

Chapter 9: Hope

Having grit depends on the hope that one's own efforts can improve the future. The gritty person must have a resolve to make tomorrow better or, as the Japanese proverb says, "Fall seven, rise eight." Conversely, pessimists have a pervasive belief that things will not get better. This is a mindset that influences everything they do, or don't do, turning minor setbacks into catastrophes. But those with gritty hope respond to setbacks with thoughts such as, "I mismanaged my time" or "I was distracted." In other words, they assess the situation and find fixable things that are temporary, specific, and surmountable. They are optimists, able to come up with creative solutions to problems. Optimism is integral to the perseverance aspect of the grit equation.

Need to Know: Hope, or optimism, can be cultivated. Cognitive behavior therapy treats pessimistic, depressive states of mind by getting people to observe their negative self-talk. We can practice reinterpreting what happens to us and respond as an optimist would, developing hope as we might any other skill.

Part III: Growing Grit from the Outside In

Chapter 10: Parenting for Grit

Developing grit does not depend only upon our internal resources. Outside influences, particularly parents, can help to raise grittier children. Families can instill interest, hope, purpose, and practice. But that doesn't mean authoritarian, demanding, "tiger" parenting, nor does it mean the type of supportive, permissive parenting that would give a child a trophy for tying their shoe. Gritty parenting borrows elements of both styles, combining compassion with the belief, trust, and expectation that a child will persist. San Francisco 49er quarterback Steve Young credits his success to a father and mother who would never let him quit. When he desperately wanted to leave college, where he'd been recruited as a quarterback and was struggling, his father told him that if he did quit, he couldn't move back home because his parents weren't going to live with a "quitter." But Young's father was not heartless, though it may sound that way. In fact, the aptly nicknamed "Grit" Young, a corporate attorney, was all about hard work and never whining, and he applied the same standards to his children, who were made to understand that you finish what you start. Without coddling, he was tremendously supportive and present for his children and tuned in to their emotional needs.

Need to Know: Tough love is not a contradiction in terms. To foster grit, parents need to enable their children's success. Teaching them it is okay to quit difficult tasks could create a negative habit that they will carry for the rest of their lives.

Chapter 11: The Playing Fields of Grit

Grit is greatly enhanced in children who participate in structured, extracurricular activities in an environment that is both supportive and demanding, be it sports, the arts, or working on the school newspaper—anything that requires commitment and practice and has a nonparent adult in charge. Duckworth knew this instinctively when she signed up her daughter for ballet classes. Pursuits like these are designed to cultivate interest, practice, purpose, and hope. The research shows that these activities have long-term payoffs on many levels, including better grades, graduation rates, career success, high self-esteem, and good behavior.

Need to Know: As soon as he or she is old enough, sign your child up for the activity of his or her choice. A child tends to thrive when a part of his week is spent doing an activity that interests him, where he can learn the principles of grit at the elbow of a wise coach or instructor.

Chapter 12: A Culture of Grit

The culture and groups in which we live shape who we are, including our grittiness. Duckworth begins with the example of the Seattle Seahawks, whose coach, Pete Carroll, has deliberately set out to build a culture of grit within his team. This same sort of philosophy can be found in the distinct cultures like West Point or the KIPP charter schools where Duckworth taught. It can be found in the companies for which we may work as adults. You know you are a part of one when you find yourself making a categorical allegiance to that group. So if you want to develop grit, seek out a gritty culture to belong to—a team in which everyone supports one another in the drive to become great competitors. Duckworth even draws on the example of a country, Finland, a tiny Nordic nation with dark, freezing winters that cherishes the notion of *sisu*, a Finnish word that means a combination of tenacity and endurance.

Need to Know: The hardest way to build grit is by yourself. Being around a lot of other gritty people will influence your character, because you will identify with members of that group. In a way, grittiness can be contagious.

Chapter 13: Conclusion

An obsession with talent distracts us from the essential truth that what we can accomplish over the course of our lifetimes depends on our grit—our passion and perseverance in achieving long-term goals. You can grow your grit from the inside out by cultivating your interests, implementing daily habits of self-improvement, and having commitment to a higher purpose. You can develop it from the outside in through a personal community of parents, teachers, bosses, mentors, friends, and teammates.

Can this lead to a happier life? Duckworth says she doesn't yet have a definitive answer to that question, but her exemplars of grit all say that when they work passionately for a purpose greater than themselves, they are thrilled. Is there ever a downside? Perhaps. There are times when sticking to something no matter what is not the right decision. Finishing whatever you begin without exception may cause you to miss out on opportunities to start other—and possibly more successful—pursuits. Still, Duckworth feels that most people would be better off with more grit, not less. She cautions that there are character traits, like morality, that matter more. But grit can help lubricate all the other strengths of will, heart, and mind. It's an integral part of a tapestry of character traits that contribute to a happy and fulfilled life.

Cast of Characters

Jeff Bezos: Founder and CEO of Amazon.com. Bezos is a believer in following your passion, and he was allowed to do so from an early age. His mother, Jackie, encouraged his tendencies toward engineering from his youngest days.

Pete Carroll: Head coach of the NFL team the Seattle Seahawks since 2010. Carroll is known for encouraging a specific culture within his team, one that he—and Duckworth—describes as gritty. When Carroll heard Duckworth's TED Talk on grit, he invited her to spend time with his team so she could watch the teaching of grit in action.

SUMMARY AND ANALYSIS

Mihaly Csikszentmihalyi: Founder of the Quality of Life Research Center. He is a well-respected psychologist known for his study of the concept of "flow," a state of intense focus. He is a Distinguished Professor of Psychology and Management at Claremont Graduate University.

Carol Dweck: Lewis and Virginia Eaton Professor at Stanford University. Dweck, a renowned psychologist, is the author of *Mindset: The New Psychology of Success*, which details the differences between fixed and growth mindsets and how they impact learning.

Anders Ericsson: Swedish cognitive psychologist noted for his studies of expertise. Ericsson, according to Duckworth, is "the world expert on world experts."

Francesca Martinez: British stand-up comedian and writer who suffers from cerebral palsy. Her parents allowed her to quit school in order to follow her passion for comedy, in spite of worries that such a field would prove too difficult for someone who is disabled. While extremely supportive of her capability to achieve her dreams, her parents nevertheless instilled in her the importance of doing the hard work that needed to be done to manage her disease.

Alex Scott: Born in Connecticut in 1996, Alex was diagnosed with neuroblastoma before she was one year old. At age four, she opened her first lemonade stand to raise money for her doctors to use in helping other sick kids. By the time she died, at age eight, Alex's Lemonade Stand had raised more than a million dollars.

Amy Wrzesniewski: Professor of Organizational Behavior at Yale. Her research focuses on how people view their occupations—in Duckworth's terms, whether they see their work as a job, a career, or a calling. Wrzesniewski has found that the specific industry has very little impact on these findings. What matters is the way the workers think of their own contributions.

Steve Young: San Francisco 49ers quarterback and MVP of Super Bowl XXIX. Duckworth describes Young as a paragon of grit. Young overcame several crises of confidence throughout his years playing at Brigham Young University and with the 49ers, eventually retiring as the highest-rated quarterback in history.

Direct Quotes and Analysis

"It was this combination of passion and perseverance that made high achievers special. In a word, they had grit."

Duckworth draws a contrast between the rising stars who drop out of a program or race and the people who don't necessarily start out as the best but stick to it, eventually winning awards and becoming highly accomplished. While our culture tends to focus on those who show early promise and natural talent, hard workers who end up having more success in the long run are often overlooked.

"Greatness is many, many individual feats, and each of them is doable."

SUMMARY AND ANALYSIS

Here, Duckworth quotes sociologist Dan Chambliss, author of a study of competitive swimmers titled "The Mundanity of Excellence," which posits that achievement is an aggregate of many smaller, reachable goals. These athletes, in Duckworth's view, demonstrate perseverance and a focus on continuous improvement that equals grit. While nobody can train to have the physical attributes of a Michael Phelps, for instance, the training itself will lead to excellence even in those without Phelps's physique.

"Talent is how quickly your skills improve when you invest effort. Achievement is what happens when you take your acquired skills and use them."

Recalling one of her earliest articles on the topic, Duckworth lays down the two simple equations that explain how individuals get from talent to achievement. She adds, though, that this concept does not consider outside forces such as opportunities, great coaches, or luck. She concedes that the psychology of success is not the complete picture.

"Staying on the treadmill is one thing, and I do think it's related to staying true to our commitments even when we're not comfortable."

Duckworth discusses the Treadmill Test, a 1940 Harvard study that asked 130 healthy young sophomore males to run on the treadmill for five minutes. The angle and speed were set to the point where the average men held on for only four minutes, and some dropped out much earlier than that. The test measured how willing the participants were to push themselves outside of their comfort zones.

"Many of us, it seems, quit what we start far too early and far too often."

Using the sports and treadmill analogy, as well as New Year's resolutions like starting vegetable gardens, knitting sweaters, or going on diets, Duckworth says that we frequently give up when we encounter the first real obstacle or plateau in progress. Quitting is easy, even though success is really just a matter of waking up the next morning and starting again.

"One moment, you have no idea what to do with your time on earth. And the next, it's all clear—you know exactly who you were meant to be."

The author talks about Julia Child's discovery of her own passion for food, which came to her later in life. This was the case for other grit paragons, as well, many of whom explored different interests before they discovered the ones that stuck with them and became their callings.

"Optimistic young adults stay healthier throughout middle age and, ultimately, live longer than pessimists."

A hopeful outlook plays an important role in gritty living. Optimism also contributes positively to one's longevity, success in marriage, school, career, etc. A pessimist might find it more logical to decide to give up, whereas an optimist might reason that if they try again, they can do better. Ergo, optimism equals grit, which equals success in broad areas of life.

"So, grit isn't everything. There are many other things a person needs in order to grow and flourish. Character is plural."

Although a proponent of growing grit, Duckworth acknowledges that it is far from being the only predictor of success. She focuses on growing character, and grit is just one piece of this. She urges readers to think about grit in terms of how it relates to these other aspects of character, which she breaks down into clusters of virtues or strengths of heart, will, and mind.

"To be gritty is to keep putting one foot in front of the other. To be gritty is to hold fast to an interesting and

purposeful goal. . . . To be gritty is to fall down seven times, and rise eight."

In reference to an old Japanese saying that Duckworth says she would tattoo on her body if she were ever so inclined. She is answering her critics, who ask whether encouraging grit does children a disservice by setting expectations unreasonably high.

Trivia

1. The first National Spelling Bee was held in 1925. The winning word, spelled by Frank Neuhauser, was *gladiolus*. In its 90th year, 2015, the spelling bee had two champions: Vanya Shivashankar and Gokul Venkatachalam.

2. In addition to strong academics and physical fitness, successful West Point applicants need a nomination from a senator, a member of congress, or the vice president of the United States.

3. Charles Darwin was one of the first of the great thinkers to touch upon the concept of grit, albeit not in so many words: "For I have always maintained that, excepting fools, men did not differ much in intellect, only in zeal and hard work; and I still think this is an *eminently* important difference."

4. Studies of identical twins are used to determine more than the inheritability of grit. Research has proven that genetics do have an influence, but there is "no single gene for grit.

5. Although the media generally describes the MacArthur Fellowship as the "genius grant," the MacArthur Foundation itself purposely never uses the word *genius*.

6. Pete Carroll, a believer in cultivating a culture of grit among his team, coached the Seattle Seahawks to their first Super Bowl win in 2014.

7. The MacArthur Foundation's "genius" fellowship is an annual prize awarded to people in varied fields who have shown extraordinary aptitude and creativity. Past fellows include writers Ta-Nehisi Coates, Jonathan Lethem, and Alison Bechdel.

8. Grit is now being taught to students in schools across the country. At KIPP, a charter school in

New York City's Washington Heights, fifth graders are taking a character class that gives them a long-term project with incremental deadlines, then asks them how they felt about the tasks and their own performance.

9. Duckworth has been working with Boston Celtics coach Brad Stevens ever since he was hired in the summer of 2013, even traveling to meet with the team for crucial games. Her grit principles directly affect how he coaches his players.

10. "John Irving, bestselling author of *The Cider House Rules* and *The World According to Garp*, has grit. An undiagnosed dyslexic, he didn't do well in school when he was young, but learned to "pay twice as much attention" and, ultimately, excel as a writer.

What's That Word?

Deliberate practice: A term coined by psychologist Anders Ericsson used to describe how high achievers practice. They focus on specific areas of improvement, set goals, and keep track of progress.

Flow: As researched and described by psychologist Mihaly Csikszentmihalyi, *flow* is a state of being that is experienced by experts during the practice of their craft. It entails a high degree of concentration that makes the experience seem almost automatic.

Flynn effect: Named after James R. Flynn, a social scientist from New Zealand who has extensively studied the topic, this term describes the continuous increase in IQ scores over the time that intelligence tests have been given. The Flynn effect is a worldwide phenomenon.

Goal hierarchies: The practice of setting a single high-level goal and then setting all other, more basic, goals to be in service of that ultimate one. Gritty people are able to keep their main goals in mind even while executing smaller, less interesting tasks, because they know those tasks are steps along the way to their true objectives.

Growth mindset: According to psychologist Carol Dweck, a growth mindset, as opposed to a fixed mindset, is a belief that intelligence can be developed. Those with a fixed mindset believe that one is born with a certain intelligence and nothing can be done to increase it.

IQ: Intelligence quotient. This is a number given based on standardized tests that purport to pinpoint a person's intelligence. Unfortunately, a low score on an IQ test can follow a child throughout his life and negatively impact the educational opportunities offered to him.

***Kaizen*:** A Japanese term meaning "change for the better." When used in the corporate arena, the term has taken on the meaning of "continuous improvement." This system of small, daily changes leading to a better outcome has inspired many business books.

Sisu: A Finnish term to describe a type of obstinate perseverance that is seen as being integral to the spirit of Finland. While *sisu* does not translate exactly to grit, it is an important component to grittiness.

Treadmill test: While a cardiac stress test usually involves jogging on a treadmill, this test refers to a study begun at Harvard University in 1940 wherein college students were asked to stay on the treadmill, set at the hardest level, for five minutes. Various psychologists followed the participants throughout their lives, tracking whether the grittiest—those who stayed on the longest—had been more successful.

Critical Response

- A *New York Times* bestseller
- A *Wall Street Journal* "Hottest Spring Nonfiction Book" of 2016
- A *Washington Post* "Leadership Book to Watch For" in 2016
- A *Forbes* "Must-Read Business Book for 2016"

"Angela Duckworth has written a contemporary classic—a clarifying and deeply researched book in the tradition of Stephen Covey and Carol Dweck. For anyone hoping to work smarter or live better, *Grit* is an essential—and perhaps life-changing—read." —Daniel H. Pink, *New York Times*–bestselling author of *Drive: The Surprising Truth About What Motivates*

SUMMARY AND ANALYSIS

"Angela Duckworth [is] the psychologist who has made 'grit' the reigning buzzword in education-policy circles. . . . Duckworth's ideas about the cultivation of tenacity have clearly changed some lives for the better. . . . In this book, Duckworth, whose TED Talk has been viewed more than eight million times, brings her lessons to the reading public."
—Judith Shulevitz,
New York Times Book Review

"*Grit* is a persuasive and fascinating response to the cult of IQ fundamentalism. Duckworth reminds us that it is character and perseverance that set the successful apart." —Malcolm Gladwell,
New York Times–bestselling author

"Impressively fresh and original. . . . *Grit* scrubs away preconceptions about how far our potential can take us. And it solves the riddle of how those not likely to succeed in fact do. Buy this, send copies to your friends, and tell the world that there *is*, in fact, hope. We can *all* dazzle." —Susan Cain,
New York Times–bestselling author of *Quiet: The Power of Introverts in a World That Can't Stop Talking*

"It really isn't talent but practice—along with passion—

that makes perfect, explains psychologist Duckworth in this illuminating book. Inspiration for non-geniuses everywhere."
—*People*

"Readable, compelling and totally persuasive. The ideas in this book have the potential to transform education, management, and the way its readers live. Angela Duckworth's *Grit* is a national treasure."
—Lawrence H. Summers,
former secretary of the treasury and
President Emeritus at Harvard University

"When I first saw Angela's TED Talk two years ago, I was hooked right away by the grit concept and how pursuing grit can lead to an optimistic, process-driven environment conducive to individual and team growth. As a coach, I'm convinced there are no more important qualities in striving for excellence than those that create true grit. Here, Angela does a great job describing those qualities. I hope you enjoy the book as much as I did." —Brad Stevens,
coach of the Boston Celtics

"This book gets into your head, which is where it belongs. Duckworth shows that, to succeed, talent (giftedness) matters, but not nearly as much as grit

SUMMARY AND ANALYSIS

(passion and persistence). She helps you figure out how much grit you have and how to develop a whole lot more of it. For educators who want our kids to succeed, this is an indispensable read." —Joel Klein, former chancellor, New York City public schools

"It's a lucid, informative, and entertaining review of the research Angela has assiduously conducted over the past decade or so. The book also includes suggestions on how to develop grit, and how we can help support grit in others." —*Scientific American*

About Angela Duckworth

A former management consultant at McKinsey, Angela Lee Duckworth left that high-powered job in her late twenties to teach math to seventh graders in the public schools of New York City, eventually teaching in San Francisco and Philadelphia as well.

The distinguished academic, who holds a degree in advanced studies neurobiology from Harvard and an MSc with distinction in neuroscience from Oxford University, has shown a lifelong commitment to education. In 1992, she founded a nonprofit summer school for low-income children that won the Better Government Award for the State of Massachusetts and was profiled as a Harvard Kennedy School case study.

After five years of teaching, she returned to graduate school to complete her PhD in psychology at the University of Pennsylvania, where she holds a position as the Christopher H. Browne Distinguished Professor of Psychology, researching concepts such as self-control and grit to determine how these traits impact success and well-being. She posits that while IQ and family income may be important to professional and academic achievement, the key factors are the qualities that make up grit, including hard work, perseverance, and the drive to improve. Her diverse research subjects include everyone from students to West Point cadets to corporate salespeople.

Dr. Duckworth has served as an advisor to presidents, CEOs, and professional sports coaches. She also cofounded the nonprofit the Character Lab with a goal of using applied research in helping educators learn how to build character in their students.

For Your Information

Online
"Angela Duckworth's book on grit has spades of appeal." Independent.com
"Don't Believe the Hype About Grit, Pleads the Scientist Behind the Concept." NYMagazine.com
"'Grit,' by Angela Duckworth." NYTimes.com
"Grit Needs Passion, Not Fear." HuffingtonPost.com
Grit: The Power of Passion and Perseverance. Ted.com
"Talent counts, but grit counts twice: best-selling author gives diversity lecture." ReviewOnline.com

Books
Grit to Great: How Perseverance, Passion, and Pluck

SUMMARY AND ANALYSIS

Take You from Ordinary to Extraordinary by Linda Kaplan Thaler and Robin Koval

How Children Succeed: Grit, Curiosity, and the Hidden Power of Character by Paul Tough

Make It Stick: The Science of Successful Learning by Peter C. Brown, Henry L. Roediger III, and Mark A. McDaniel

Mindset: The New Psychology of Success by Carol S. Dweck

Peak: Secrets from the New Science of Expertise by Anders Ericsson

The Road to Character by David Brooks

Bibliography

"Ability, zeal and capacity for hard labor,": Charles Darwin, Letter to Francis Galton, December 23, 1869. Frederick Burkhardt et al., ed., *The Correspondence of Charles Darwin*, vol. 17, 1869. Cambridge, UK: Cambridge University Press.

"Better Government Award," Penn Arts & Sciences, Positive Psychology Center, https://ppc.sas.upenn.edu/people/angela-duckworth.

Chambliss, Daniel F. "The Mundanity of Excellence: An Ethnographic Report on Stratification and Olympic Swimmers," *Sociological Theory* 7 (1989): 70–86.

"Character Lab," Angela Duckworth web page, http://angeladuckworth.com/

SUMMARY AND ANALYSIS

"Christopher H. Browne Distinguished Professor," Penn Arts & Sciences, Psychology, https://psychology.sas.upenn.edu/people/angela-duckworth.

Duckworth, Angela Lee. "Teach math to seventh graders," Last modified May 2013, https://www.ted.com/speakers/angela_lee_duckworth.

WORTH BOOKS
SMART SUMMARIES

So much to read, so little time?

Explore summaries of bestselling fiction and essential nonfiction books on a variety of subjects, including business, history, science, lifestyle, and much more.

Visit the store at
www.ebookstore.worthbooks.com

MORE SMART SUMMARIES
FROM WORTH BOOKS

POPULAR SCIENCE

MORE SMART SUMMARIES
FROM WORTH BOOKS

SELF-IMPROVEMENT

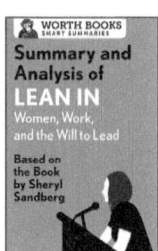

EARLY BIRD BOOKS
FRESH EBOOK DEALS, DELIVERED DAILY

LOVE TO READ?
LOVE GREAT SALES?

GET FANTASTIC DEALS ON BESTSELLING EBOOKS DELIVERED TO YOUR INBOX EVERY DAY!

Find a full list of our authors and
titles at www.openroadmedia.com

FOLLOW US
@OpenRoadMedia

www.ingramcontent.com/pod-product-compliance
Lightning Source LLC
Chambersburg PA
CBHW060343080526
44584CB00013B/897